BRAIN ACADEMY
English

MISSION FILE 2

Years 3-4

Angie Walker

Produced in association with

National Association
for Able Children
in Education

Rising Stars are grateful to the following people for their support in developing this series: Sue Mordecai, Julie Fitzpatrick, Johanna Raffan and Belle Wallace.

NACE, PO Box 242, Arnolds Way, Oxford OX2 9FR
www.nace.co.uk

Rising Stars UK Ltd, 22 Grafton Street, London W1S 4EX
www.risingstars-uk.com

Every effort has been made to trace copyright holders and obtain their permission for the use of copyright materials. The authors and publisher will gladly receive information enabling them to rectify any error or omission in subsequent editions.

All facts are correct at time of going to press.

Published 2008
Text, design and layout © Rising Stars UK Ltd.

Mission challenges and character speech written by Richard Cooper
Think Tanks written by Rachel Beyer
Project Management: Deborah Kespert
Cover design: Burville-Riley Design
Design: Pentacorbig
Background image on Mission pages: © zphoto – Fotolia.com
Illustrations: Cover – Burville-Riley Design / Characters – Bill Greenhead

All rights reserved. No part of this publication may be reproduced, stored in a retrieval system, or transmitted, in any form by any means, electronic, mechanical, photocopying, recording or otherwise, without the prior permission of Rising Stars.

British Library Cataloguing in Publication Data.
A CIP record for this book is available from the British Library.

ISBN: 978-1-84680-363-5

Printed by Craft Print International Ltd, Singapore

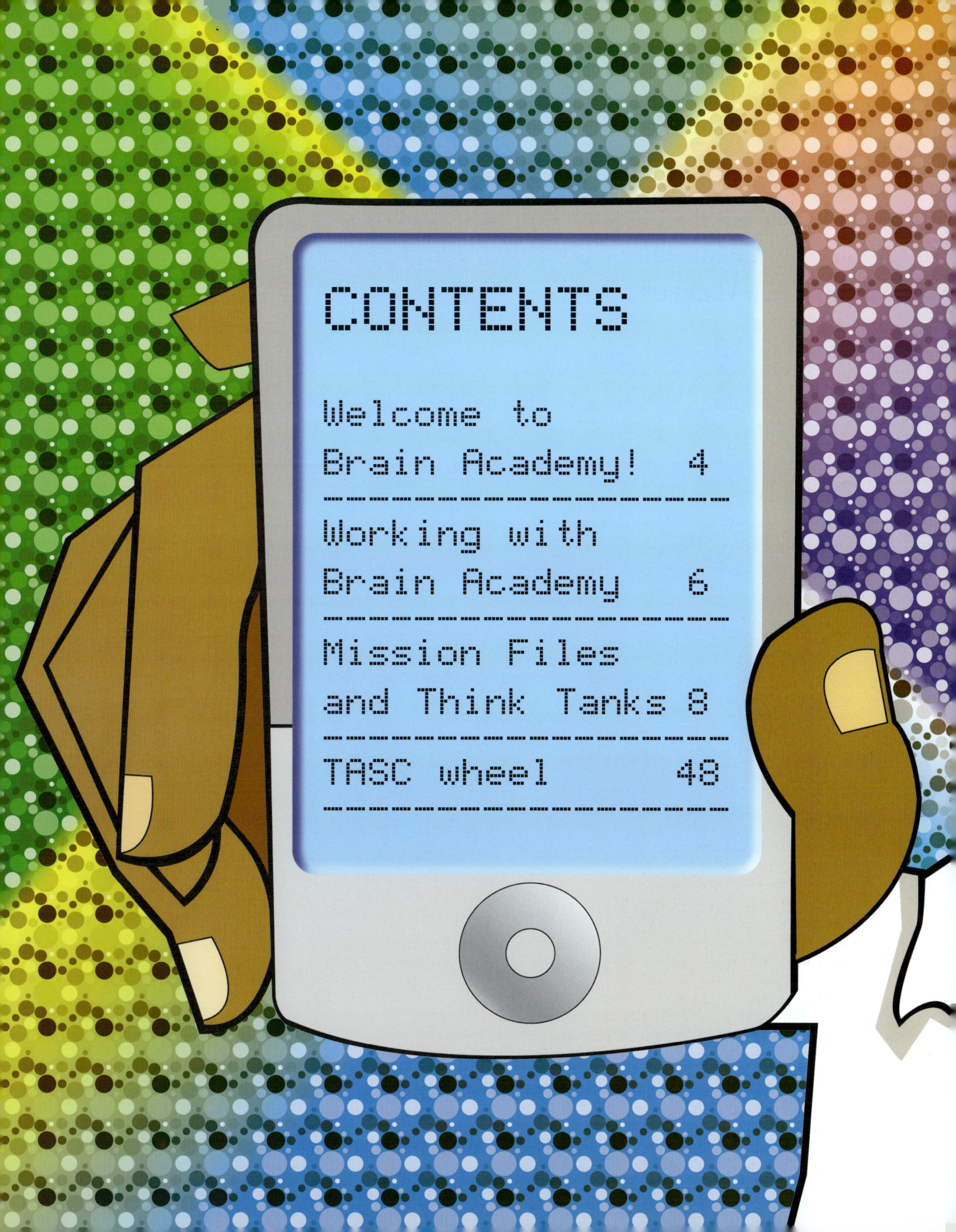

Welcome to Brain Academy!

Welcome to Brain Academy! Make yourself at home. We are here to give you the low-down on the organisation – so pay attention!

It's our job to help Da Vinci and his colleagues to solve the tough problems they face and we would like you to join us as members of the Academy. Are you up to the challenge?

Da Vinci
Da Vinci is the founder and head of the Brain Academy. He is all seeing, all thinking and all knowing – possibly the cleverest person alive. Nobody has ever actually seen him in the flesh as he communicates only via computer. When Da Vinci receives an emergency call for help, the members of Brain Academy jump into action (and that means you!).

Huxley
Huxley is Da Vinci's right-hand man. Not as clever, but still very smart. He is here to guide you through the missions and offer help and advice. The sensible and reliable face of Brain Academy, Huxley is cool under pressure.

Dr Hood
The mad doctor is the arch-enemy of Da Vinci and Brain Academy. He has set up a rival organisation called D.A.F.T. (which stands for Dull And Feeble Thinkers). Dr Hood and his agents will do anything they can to irritate and annoy the good people of this planet. He is a pain we could do without.

Hilary Kumar
Ms Kumar is the Prime Minister of our country. As the national leader she has a hotline through to the Academy but will only call in an extreme emergency. Confident and strong willed, she is a very tough cookie indeed.

General Cods-Wallop
This highly decorated gentleman (with medals, not wallpaper) is in charge of the armed forces. Most of his success has come from the help of Da Vinci and the Academy rather than the use of his somewhat limited military brain.

Mrs Tiggles
Stella Tiggles is the retired head of the Secret Intelligence service. She is a particular favourite of Da Vinci who treats her as his own mother. Mrs Tiggles' faithful companion is her cat, Bond … James Bond.

PICKFORD & BLACK

Partners Robert Pickford (1841-1914) and William A Black (1847-1934) were ship chandlers and grocers of Halifax, Nova Scotia. Pickford founded the business in 1870, and Black joined the firm in 1878, which was still flourishing in 1929.

The firm expanded into shipping and steamships and into the West Indies trade. They acquired Seeton's Wharf at Halifax, Nova Scotia and by 1877 they had purchased the Cunard Line ships *ALPHA* and *BETA*, establishing a shipping service between Halifax, Cuba and Bermuda by 1889. They also ran steamship services in the Atlantic provinces.

The company became Pickford & Black Ltd when Robert Pickford retired in 1911. The firm was also an agent for Lloyd's and other major European steamship lines. In 1975 it became a wholly-owned subsidiary of McLean Kennedy Limited and in 2002 a branch of F K Warren.

Coffee cup and egg cup.

Large silver plated tureen with lid.

QUEBEC STEAMSHIP COMPANY

The Quebec Steamship Company was founded in 1867 to provide shipping services to the Canadian east coast maritime and inland provinces, of the new Canadian Federation. The line was originally named the Quebec and Gulf Ports Steamship Company and benefitted from a government subsidy. In 1874 the company obtained a subsidy from the Bermuda Government to provide a three weekly service from New York to Bermuda, initially the service being primarily for cargo and only a few passengers were carried. The first sailing was made by the small steamer **CANIMA** in January 1874. In 1877 an additional contract was obtained from the Venezuelan Government to provide a service from New York to the Venezuelan ports of Puerto Cabello and La Guaira. This contract was short lived and cancelled after a couple of years, following a revolution in Venezuela.

The houseflag of the Quebec Steamship Company.

The company then decided to develop services from New York to the West Indian Windward and Leeward Islands, Venezuela, Demerera and Trinidad and from New York north to New Brunswick and Nova Scotia. As a result of the new services, the company became the Quebec Steamship Company in 1880.

Scallop shaped dish manufactured for the company by John Maddock & Sons Limited.

"We were just like you once – ordinary schoolchildren leading ordinary lives. Then one day we all received a call from a strange character named Da Vinci. From that day on, we have led a double life – as secret members of Brain Academy!"

"Here are a few things you should know about the people you'll meet on your journey."

Echo the Eco-Warrior
Echo is the hippest chick around. Her love of nature and desire for justice will see her do anything to help an environmental cause – even if it means she's going to get her clothes dirty.

Buster Crimes
Buster is a really smooth dude and is in charge of the Police Force. His laid-back but efficient style has won him many friends, although these don't include Dr Hood or the agents of D.A.F.T. who regularly try to trick the coolest cop in town.

Maryland T. Wordsworth
M.T. Wordsworth is the president of the USA. Not the sharpest tool in the box, Maryland prefers to be known by his middle name, Texas, or 'Tex' for short. He takes great exception to being referred to as 'Mary' (which has happened in the past).

Prince Barrington
Prince Barrington, or 'Bazza' as he is known to his friends, is the publicity-seeking heir to the throne. Always game for a laugh, the Prince will stop at nothing to raise money for worthy causes. A 'good egg' as his mother might say.

Victor Blastov
Victor Blastov is the leading scientist at the Space Agency. He once tried to build a rocket by himself but failed to get the lid off the glue. Victor often requires the services of the Academy, even if it's to set the video to record Dr Who.

Sandy Buckett
The fearless Sandy Buckett is the head of the fire service. Sandy and her team of brave firefighters are always on hand, whether to extinguish the flames of chaos caused by the demented Dr Hood or just to rescue Mrs Tiggles' cat …

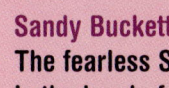

5

Working with Brain Academy

Do you get the idea? Now you've had the introduction we are going to show you the best way to use this book.

The Challenge
The team tells you what the mission is about.

The Training Mission
Here you will get some practice before being sent on the Main Mission.

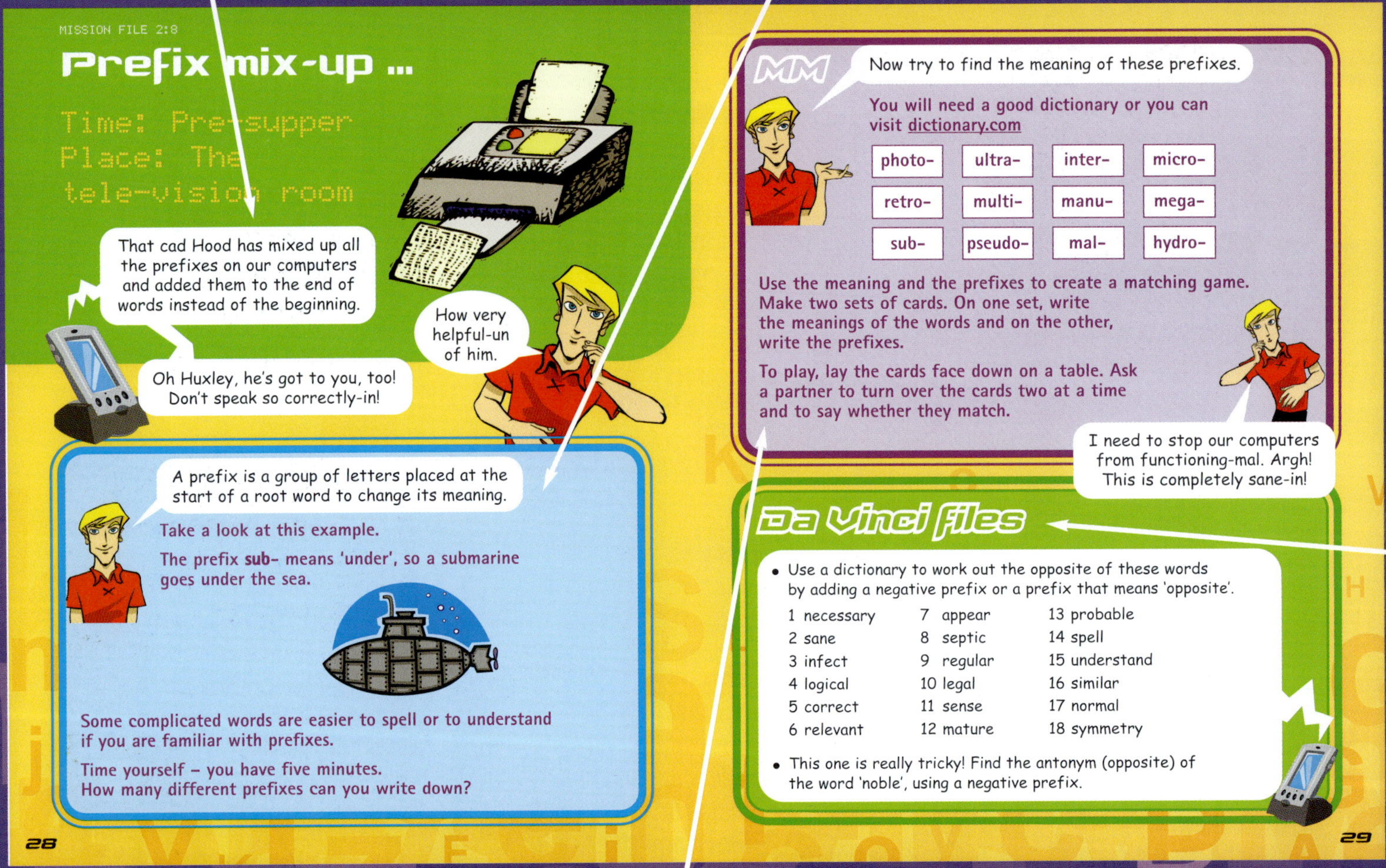

MISSION FILE 2:8
Prefix mix-up ...
Time: Pre-supper
Place: The tele-vision room

That cad Hood has mixed up all the prefixes on our computers and added them to the end of words instead of the beginning.

How very helpful-un of him.

Oh Huxley, he's got to you, too! Don't speak so correctly-in!

A prefix is a group of letters placed at the start of a root word to change its meaning.

Take a look at this example.

The prefix **sub-** means 'under', so a submarine goes under the sea.

Some complicated words are easier to spell or to understand if you are familiar with prefixes.

Time yourself – you have five minutes.
How many different prefixes can you write down?

MM Now try to find the meaning of these prefixes.

You will need a good dictionary or you can visit <u>dictionary.com</u>

photo-	ultra-	inter-	micro-
retro-	multi-	manu-	mega-
sub-	pseudo-	mal-	hydro-

Use the meaning and the prefixes to create a matching game. Make two sets of cards. On one set, write the meanings of the words and on the other, write the prefixes.

To play, lay the cards face down on a table. Ask a partner to turn over the cards two at a time and to say whether they match.

I need to stop our computers from functioning-mal. Argh! This is completely sane-in!

Da Vinci files

- Use a dictionary to work out the opposite of these words by adding a negative prefix or a prefix that means 'opposite'.

1 necessary	7 appear	13 probable
2 sane	8 septic	14 spell
3 infect	9 regular	15 understand
4 logical	10 legal	16 similar
5 correct	11 sense	17 normal
6 relevant	12 mature	18 symmetry

- This one is really tricky! Find the antonym (opposite) of the word 'noble', using a negative prefix.

The Main Mission
This is where you try to complete the challenge.

The crest of the Quebec Steamship Company used on its china in the latter part of the 19th century.

The most important route to the company became the one from New York to Bermuda, in particular the carriage of passengers and larger vessels were employed on the route with greater passenger capacity, for example **TRINIDAD** (1884 - 180 passengers) and **BERMUDIAN** (1905 - 340 passengers).

Large water pitcher used by the line in the 20th century.

In 1913 the company was taken over by Canada Steamship Lines and both of the liners employed on the route from New York were taken over for Government service during the First World War, the **BERMUDIAN** as a troopship, being sunk in the harbour of Alexandria (but refloated and later returned to the company) and the **TRINIDAD** was torpedoed by a U-boat in 1918. At the time of the armistice three cargo ships had survived and these three ships and the **BERMUDIAN** and other assets of the company were acquired by Furness Withy Ltd from Canada Steamship Lines in 1919. Furness Withy also purchased the Trinidad Shipping and Trading Company in 1920 and the two companies were amalgamated in 1920 to form the Bermuda and West Indies Steamship Company - the famous Furness Bermuda Line.

SOURCES OF INFORMATION AND SELECTED BIBLIOGRAPHY

Encyclopaedia of British Pottery & Porcelain Marks - Geoffrey A Godden, Barrie & Jenkins, London

Houseflags
Lloyd's List of House Flags published in 1882
Lloyd's Book of House Flag & Funnels published in 1904 and 1912
Flags National & Mercantile House Flags & Funnels by Griffin & Company, Portsmouth
S. S. House Flags and *Reed's Flags and Funnels* by Thomas Reed & Co Ltd, Sunderland
Brown's Flags & Funnels (nine editions) by Brown, Son & Ferguson Ltd
Glasgow Flags, Funnels and Hull Colours published by Adlard Coles Limited
Charts depicting House Flags & Funnels published by the Liverpool Journal of Commerce
House-Flags and Funnels of British and Foreign Shipping Companies drawn and edited by E C Talbot-Booth in 1937
A Survey of Mercantile Houseflags & Funnels by J L Loughran, published by Waine Research Publications in 1979

General
Merchant Fleets in Profile by Duncan Haws - Patrick Stephens, Cambridge
Merchant Fleets by Duncan Haws - TCL Publications, Hereford
South Atlantic Seaway by N R P Bonsor - Brookside Publications, Jersey, Channel Islands
Travels of the Tramps (five volumes) by Norman L Middlemiss - Shield Publications, North Shields
Records by Ships in Focus Publications, Preston
Passenger Ships of Australia & New Zealand (two volumes), Peter Plowman   Conway Maritime, Greenwich
British Ocean Tramps - Volume 2. Owners & Their Ships by P N Thomas   Waine Research Publications
Coastal & Short Sea Liners by C V Waine, Waine Research Publications, Wolverhampton
Steam Coasters by C V Waine, Waine Research Publications, Wolverhampton
Transpacific Steam by E Mowbrat Tate
The Vanished Fleet by T K Fitchett, Rigby, Adelaide
Australian Ships by Gillett, Child & Associates Pty Ltd, Australia

Periodicals and Magazines
Ships Monthly Magazine, Burton on Trent
Sea Breezes Magazine, Douglas, Isle of Man
Shipping Today and Yesterday Magazine, St Leonards on Sea
Ships in Focus Publications, Preston

Shipping Company Histories
Anchor Line 1856-1956 by R S McLellan - Company 1956
Anchor Ships and Anchor Men (Anchor Shipping & Foundry Co) Reed, Wellington & Auckland
Adelaide SS Co. Fitted for the Voyage by Michael Paige, Rigby, Adelaide
Australian Commonwealth Shipping Line by Frank Brennan   Roebuck Society, Canberra
Black Ball Line of Packets - The Passage Makers by Michael Stammers - Teredo Books Ltd, Brighton, Sussex
Blue Funnel - A history of Alfred Holt & Company 1865-1914 by Francis E Hyde - Liverpool University Press
The Blue Funnel Legend - A History of the Ocean Steam Ship Company 1865-1973 by Malcolm Falkus Macmillan, London

B.I Centenary 1856-1956 - The Story of the British India Steam Navigation Co Ltd by George Blake, Collins, London

B I - The British India Steam Navigation Company Limited by W A Laxon & F W Perry - World Ship Society

The Lady Boats - The Life & Times of Canada's West Indies Merchant Fleet by Felicity Hanington - Canadian Marine Transportation Centre, Dalhousie University

Canadian Pacific The Story of the Famous Shipping Line by George Musk - David & Charles, Newton Abbott

The China Navigation Company Limited - A pictorial History 1872-1992, published by Butterfield & Swire/ John Swire & Sons, London

Furness Withy 1891-1991 by David Burrell - World Ship Society

Clipper Ship to Motor Liner - The story of the New Zealand Shipping Company 1873-1939 by Sydney D Waters - company publication

Crossed Flags - The Histories of the New Zealand Shipping Company - Federal Steam Navigation Company and their subsidiaries by W A Laxon, I J Farquhar, N J Kirby & F W Perry - World Ship Society

Steam Conquers the Pacific by Arthur C Wardle

Port Line by H C Spong & J Dobson - World Ship Society

Port Line The Tyser Legacy, Farquhar New Zealand Ship & Marine Society, Wellington

Union Line - A short history of the Union Steam Ship Company of New Zealand Limited 1875-1951 by Sydney D Waters, Company publication

Union Fleet by Ian Farquhar (Union Steam Ship Company of New Zealand) New Zealand Ship & Marine Soc. (Inc), Wellington

Libraries and Museums
The Caird Library, National Maritime Museum, Greenwich, London
Public Records Office, Kew, London

The Ships List
Wikipedia

INDEX OF COMPANIES IN VOLUME 4

Numbers in **BOLD** refer to the pages where an article on a specific company history is located

Adelaide Steamship Co Ltd	**86**,87
Adsteam Marine	88
African & Eastern Trade Corporation Ltd	60
African Steamship Co	7
Alfred Holt & Co	48,84
Allan Line	2,7
American Line	19
Anchor Line	14,19
Anchor Shipping and Foundry Company Limited, Nelson	**89**,102
Anglo-Australasian Steam Navigation Co	75
Asiatic Steam Navigation Co	52
Associated Steamships Ltd	88
Austin Friars Steamship Co	29
Australian & Eastern Steam Navigation Co	16
Australian Oriental Line	**94**
Australasian Steam Navigation Co	**90**
Australasian United Steam Navigation Co Ltd (AUSN)	**92**
B & S Shipping Co Ltd	76
Bank Line	8
Barber Steamship Lines	49
Barrow Steamship Co	14
Barry Shipping Co	76,77
Basra Steam Shipping Co	29
Bermuda & West Indies Steamship Co	105
Birkenhead Shipping Co	50
Bitumen & Oil Refineries Australia Ltd	99
Black Ball Line of Packets	**15**,16
Blue Funnel Line	2,41,48,84
Bombay & Persia Steam Navigation Co	52
Booth Line	65,66
Booth Iquitos Steamship Co Ltd	65
Booth Steamship Co (1901) Ltd	66
Bowater Steamship Co Ltd	**17**,18
Bristol City Line	33,41
British & African Steam Navigation Co	7,99
British & American Steam Navigation Co	8
British & Commonwealth Shipping Co	8,18,20
British & Foreign Steam Ship Co	60,64
British & North American Royal Mail Steam Packet Co Ltd	50,58
British India Steam Navigation Co	2,8,35,52,91,92
British Shipowners Co Ltd	**19**
Bromport Steamship Co	60
Bullard King & Co (Natal Line of Steamers)	**20**
Burns, Philp & Co Ltd	94,**95**
Cairn Line of Steamers	64
Canada Ocean Steam Ship Co	24
Canada Steamship Lines	105

Canadian & Australian Royal Mail Line	98
Canadian Northern Steamship Co	23
Canadian Pacific	2
Charente Steamship Co	7
Chilean Line	7
China Coastal Steam Navigation Co	40
China Navigation Co	11,94
Clan Line	8,20
Coast Steamships Ltd	87,88
Colonial & Union Co	75
Commonwealth and Dominion Line	41,75
Compañia Sudamericana de Vapores	7
County Steam Ship Co	44
Cunard Steamship Co	2
Dalgleish Ltd, R S	**22**
David MacIver & Co	51
David MacIver Sons & Co	50
Delmas Vieljeux	61
Dominion Line	56
Dundee, Perth & London Shipping Co	8,30
Dundee & Hull Steam Packet Co	8
Eastern Steam Navigation Co	8
Egyptian Mail Steamship Co Ltd	**23**
Elder Dempster Lines	2,7,61,99
Ellerman & Papayanni Lines Ltd	44
Ellerman's Wilson Line	3
European and Australian Royal Mail Co	**24**
European & Colombian Steam Navigation Co	24
Euxine Shipping Co Ltd	**26**
Evan Thomas, Radcliffe & Co	**27**,28
Federal Wharf Co Ltd	86
French Line	2
Furness Bermuda Line	8
Furness Lines	19
Furness, Withy & Co	17,45,82,83,105
Galbraith, Pembroke & Co	**29**
Galbraith, Stringer, Pembroke & Co	29
George Gibson & Co Ltd	**30**
George Milne & Company (Inver Line)	32
Ghana Black Star Line	61
Gibbs, Bright & Co	16
Gibson Gas Carriers Ltd	31
Gibson-Rankine Line	31
Glen Line	2
Globe Shipping Co	**55**
Gowland Steam Ship Co	38
Graig Shipping Co, Cardiff	29
Great Western Steamship Co	**33**
Guinea Gulf Line	61
Guion Line	82

Gulf Transport Line (J H Welshford & Co)	**34**
Hain Nourse Line Ltd	36
Hain Steamship Co Ltd	**35**
Halifax & West India Steamship Co	58
Hamilton, Fraser & Co (Inch Line)	39
Harrison, J & C Ltd	**37**
Harrison Ltd, T & J	7,64
Head Line	79
Herron, Dunn & Co	55
Heyn & Sons Ltd, G	78,80
Holman, J	62
Houlder Brothers	7,77
Howard Smith	88,101
Huddart Parker Ltd	**97**
Hunter River Steam Navigation Co	90,92
Inch Shipping Co Ltd	39
Indo-China Steam Navigation Co	**40**
Indra Line (Thos B Royden & Co)	**41**,75
Iquitos Steamship Co Ltd	65
Iredale & Porter, P	**59**
Irish Shipowners Co Ltd	**80**
Isthmian Steamship Line	56
Jamaica Banana Producers Steamship Co	43
Jamaica Direct Fruit Line/Jamaica Banana Steamship Co	**42**
Jamaica Merchant Marine Atlantic Line	42
Jamaica Producers Steamship Co	42
Japp & Kirby	**44**
Japp, Hatch & Co London	44
Jardine, Matheson & Co	40
Jardine Ship Management Ltd	40
Johnston Line (William & Edmund Johnston)	**45**,50
Johnston Warren Line	45,83
Khedivial Mail Line	**46**
Khedivial Mail Steamship & Graving Dock Co	46,93
Knight Line (Greenshields, Cowie & Company)	**48**
Lancashire Shipping Co (James Chambers & Co)	**49**
Lancaster Shipping Co	49
Leyland Line	84
London & Edinburgh Steam Packet Co	8
Lord Line	79,80
MacIver Line	50
Markland Shipping Co	17
McIlwraith McEacharn & Co	88
McLean Kennedy Ltd	103
Melbourne Coal, Shipping & Engineering Co	100,101
Melbourne Shipping Co Ltd	101
Melbourne Steamship Co	**100**
Mercantile Steam Ship Co	36

Miller & Co, R W	
Mitchell Cotts & Co	64
Mogul Line Ltd	**52**
Møller-Maersk, A P	83
Mondrich Steam Ship Co	44
Monkswood Shipping Co Ltd	76
Morison & Co , John	**53**
Mossgiel Steamship Co Ltd (J Bruce & Co Glasgow)	**54**
Mudie, R A & Mudie, J H	81
National Steamship Co	37
Nelson Line	42
New York & South America Line	**55**
New Zealand & Australia Steamship Co	98
New York & South America Line	**55**
New Zealand Shipping Co	2,8,19
Nicholson & Co, J	**57**
Niger Company	60
Nigerian National Shipping Line	61
Northern Steam Ship Co, Auckland	**102**
Nova Scotia, Newfoundland and Bermuda Royal Mail Steam Packet Co	**58**
Ocean Transport & Trading Co (Ocean Fleets/Blue Funnel Line)	61
Orient Line	2,8
Orient Steam Navigation Co	12
P&O	2
P&O Orient Line	8
Pacific Steam Navigation Co	2,7,8
Palm Line	**60**
Peninsular & Oriental Steam Navigation Co	35,46
Pharaonic Mail Line	46
Pickford & Black, Canada	**103**
Planet Line	**62**
Pool Shipping Co	72
Port Line	75
Pollok, Gilmour & Co	63
Port Adelaide Dredging Co	86
Quebec & Gulf Ports Steamship Co	104
Quebec Steamship Co	**104**,105
Queensland Steam Shipping Co	90,92
Rankin, Gilmour & Co Ltd	63
Red Cross Iquitos Steamship Co	65
Red Cross Line	65,66
Red Cross Line of Steamers to Northern Ports of Brazil (R Singlehurst & Co)	**65**
Redcroft SN Co Ltd (Lewis Lougher)	67
Rio Grande Do Sul Shipping Co Ltd	68
Robert Rankin & Co (Saint John, New Brunswick)	63
Ropner & Co	**72**
Ropner & Pool Shipping Co	73
Ropner Shipping Co	72

Rover Shipping Co	39
Royal Exchange Shipping Co Ltd (The Monarch Line)	**70**
Royal Mail Steam Packet Co	8,24,50,51
Santa Clara Steam Ship Co	41
Shakespear Shipping Co	77
Shaw, Savill & Albion	2,19
Singlehurst& Co, R	65
South African Marine Corp, (Safmarine)	21
South American Saint Line	**76**,77
Southern Whaling and Sealing Co	60
Spencer's Gulf Shipping Co Ltd	86
Springbok Shipping Co	21
St Quentin Shipping Co Ltd	76,77
Star Line Limited (James P Corry)	74
Strick Lines	36
Tasmanian Steamers Proprietary Ltd	98
Transatlantic Steamship Co	8
Triton Steamship Co	77
Tyser Line	75
Ulster Steamship Company Ltd (G Heyn & Sons Ltd)	79,80
Union-Castle Mail Steamship Co	2,3,8,20,21
Union Steam Ship Co Ltd	34,**78**,89,98,102
Union Steam Ship Co of New Zealand	9,98
United Africa Co Ltd	60
United Arab Maritime Co	47
US Steel Products Co	56
Village SS Co Ltd (R A Mudie & J H Mudie)	81
Warren Line	45,82
Watergate Steam Ship Co Ltd	22
Welshford, J H & Co	62
West India & Pacific Steamship Co	**84**
White Diamond Steamship Co Ltd	82
White Star Line	2,11,12,16
White Star Line of Boston Packets	49
William Cory & Son Ltd	37
Willis Steam Ship Co	38

Each book contains a number of Missions and Think Tanks. You will work with the characters in the Brain Academy to complete these challenges.

Each mission is divided up into different parts.

No one said this was easy. In fact, that is why you have been chosen. Da Vinci will only take the best and he believes that includes you. Good luck!

The Think Tank
In the Think Tank, Da Vinci sets a scene for you to consider. You'll need to look at it from different points of view and give your own opinion. There is no right or wrong answer in the Think Tank, only choices!

The Da Vinci Files
These problems are for the best Brain Academy recruits. Very tough. Are you tough enough?

THINK TANK 1

Why do people argue?

It's time for you to head into the Think Tank. Da Vinci has set a problem for you. He wants you to think about what makes people argue, so put on your virtual reality helmet and follow the scene carefully ...

Brothers

Harvey grinned to himself. He knew when Dennis found out what he had done he would be in big trouble but, right now, he didn't care.

Dennis received the game for his birthday. It was a game that Harvey had wanted too but Dennis was being so spiteful that he had only let Harvey play with it once so far – it wasn't fair! If Dennis wasn't going to let him play, Harvey decided that he was going to help himself.

Carefully sneaking into his brother's room, he took the game, quiet as a mouse. He hurried back, half closed the door, then waited and listened.

"Mum!" he heard Dennis shout, "Harvey's been in my room again." Mum sighed. The boys were always arguing and she was fed up with the noise. Harvey closed the door and stepped back towards his bed. He heard a crunch. The game!

In his rush, Harvey had flung the game on the floor of his room before closing the door just enough to hear what was going on. He turned round. The game was in pieces.
Now Dennis would be really mad.

Harvey stood with his back against the door. His heart pounded as he waited to see what would happen next ...

> Sometimes, people in the same house find it hard to get on. Brothers and sisters often argue about little things. The arguments can be short or go on for weeks!

> Sharing toys or rooms can cause an argument. But nothing can change the fact that brothers and sisters are related to one another and at times, will have to get on.

Talk about it

- What makes brothers and sisters argue?
- When do brothers and sisters get on with each other?
- Do you think what Harvey did was right?
- What do you think his Mum will do?
- How do you imagine Dennis will react when he finds out what has happened?
- How would you feel if you were Dennis?
- Have you ever been in an argument with your brother, sister or friend? What caused the argument?
- How do people feel when they argue?

Write about it

- Thought shower things people argue about.
- Thought track Harvey's feelings from stealing the game to breaking it. What might happen next?
- List things people could do to stop themselves from getting into an argument.

Act it

- Dennis coming to find Harvey.
- Mum talking to Harvey and Dennis about what has happened.

MISSION FILE 2:1

Adverb-isements?

```
Time: TV-time
Place: White House living room
```

"My favourite TV shows are those funny adverbs between the programmes. The best one is that lil' ol' bear doin' his silly dance selling toothpaste!"

"Adverbs on TV? Dancing bears? I think you mean adverts, Tex!"

TM

"Can you help Tex recognise an adverb? Let's start with some games."

Thought shower adverbs ending in **-ly**, e.g. *silently, softly*. Use a dictionary and a thesaurus to help you.

Make up a quiz where the aim is to find the adverb antonyms (opposites). Write lists of adverbs and ask a partner to underline the opposites.

E.g. 1 <u>frequently</u>, lonely, rapidly, <u>rarely</u>

2 <u>slowly</u>, cautiously, <u>quickly</u>, pompously

Play this game. Choose an adverb, e.g. *frantically*. Ask your friends to think of three actions, e.g. *clean your teeth, sing, walk*. Act out the actions including the adverb while your friends guess what it is.

Take a look at the table below. What spelling rules do you notice?

suspiciously	furiously	dozily	comically
tragically	carefully	defiantly	romantically
deftly	anxiously	edgily	arrogantly
haughtily	sullenly	swiftly	nonchalantly
viciously	mercilessly	gloomily	magically

Why do you think there are different endings for certain words, e.g. *-ily, -ally, -ly*?

Can you guess the meaning of any words you don't know? Check in a dictionary. Try saying sentences to a partner using the adverbs above correctly.

Gee! You *thoughtfully* told me what an abverb is.

- Write a short poem starting with single adverbs marked off by a comma. The subject is the weather. Here's an example.

  *Swiftly, the sun is upon us again,
  Dreamily, the heat rolls over me,
  Gloomily, heavy clouds bearing storms approach.*

- Make sure you use a comma at the end of each line, except for the last line.

MISSION FILE 2:2

I will give to you ...

```
Time: Echo's birthday
Place: The animal sanctuary
```

What are you going to buy me for my birthday, Sandy?

I'll give you a poem which you can keep forever.

(Sigh.) Gosh! Thanks, Sandy ...

 TM To make any kind of writing more interesting, you can use compound and complex sentences.

Compound sentences are joined by co-ordinating connectives, e.g. *and*, *but*, *so*.

Complex sentences are joined by subordinating connectives, e.g. *because*, *if*.

Thought shower as many connectives as you can.

Your mission is to write a 'gift' poem using precise language.

Each line should use a compound sentence with a comma followed by 'so'. Make sure you give a reason for the gift each time. Take a look at these examples.

I will give to you the horns of Taurus, so you will rule the land.

I will give to you the patience of a tortoise, so nothing will get in your way.

Think about precise gifts you could give to someone special. Here are some ideas:

- objects belonging to gods such as the white feather of Anubis, or the sword of Blackbeard
- animal characteristics, e.g. *the speed of a cheetah*
- natural forces such as the power of the wind
- natural objects, e.g. *the rarest, most precious diamond from under Vesuvius*
- mythological creatures
- planets

Sandy also adopted a rare turtle for me. I've named it after her!

Da Vinci files

- Try writing more complex sentences based around your gifts by replacing 'so' with these subordinating connectives: although, because, if, when.

    E.g. *I will give you the eyes of Tiresias, when you need to foretell the future.*

MISSION FILE 2:3

A dragon, by George!

Time: For a hero
Place: The BA rooftops

"Hood has sent a mighty dragon to come and destroy us all. Help!"

"Tally-ho! I'll give the overgrown lizard what for with my anti-dragon missiles. FIRE!"

"Your mission is to analyse the painting *Saint George and the Dragon* by Paolo Uccello."

You can find it in the Previous Pictures section at www.takeonepicture.org

Describe what is happening to a partner.

Consider these features of myths and legends:

- battles and quests
- gory, dramatic language
- themes such as good versus evil, heroes following their fate, danger
- faraway and timeless settings
- objects such as swords
- stereotypical characters that provide a quick identity but ignore the uniqueness of individuals

Talk about how this painting is typical of the legend genre.

14

Write a dialogue about what the people might say before and after the dragon is defeated.

Use these tips to help you.

- Start a new line for each speaker and include inverted commas around the direct speech (words spoken).

  Keep punctuation inside the inverted commas, including capital letters for the start of a sentence.

  Use a comma between the direct speech and the speech tag (the phrase telling you who is speaking), unless you need a question or exclamation mark.

  E.g. *"You will harm no one else," called the brave knight.*

- Vary the dialogue by moving speech tags in front of the direct speech, e.g. *The brave knight called, "You will harm no one else."*

- Add an action to the speech tag to show the character's personality, e.g. *"You will harm no one else," called the brave knight, thrusting his lance into the fearsome dragon.*

Da Vinci files

- Change the characters in the painting to make them seem less like stereotypes. Perhaps George could be hesitant and scared. Rewrite your dialogue based on these new character traits.
- Turn your dialogue into a poem or a story. Challenge another stereotype by showing sympathy for the dragon.

MISSION FILE 2:4

That Cinquain feeling ...

Time: A sunny Sunday
Place: The boating lake

This is the life, relaxing with a row around the lake.

Huxley, there's water coming in. I don't want to get my hard drive wet!

Whoa! There's a hole in the bottom of the boat. I'll get bailing!

TM Search for the painting *A Sunday Afternoon on the Island of la Grande Jatte* by George Seurat on the Internet. Type in 'Seurat, Sunday afternoon'.

Thought shower ideas for a one-word title. Why did you choose this title?

Thought shower adjectives to describe the scene, e.g. *still, peaceful*.

Thought shower action verbs to show what the people are doing, e.g. *daydreaming, lazing*.

Track the daydreams of one character. Are they alone or with family or friends? Write a postcard home from this person.

Print out the picture and create a display showing the thoughts of different characters.

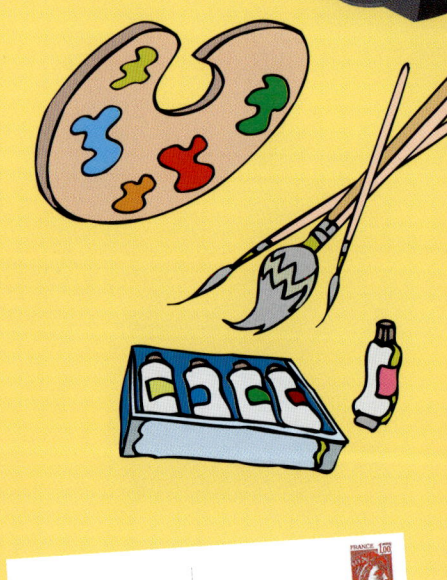

 A cinquain is a five-line poem that describes a place or thing. Here is an example.

Summer
Hot, endless
Lazing, dreaming, watching
Children play around us
Bliss!

Written down, it has a diamond shape. Try writing a cinquain based on Seurat's painting. Each line should follow this recipe.

Line 1   Write one word that sums up the subject and could be the poem's title.

Line 2   Write two adjectives that describe the subject.

Line 3   Write three action verbs ending in **-ing** that tell what is happening.

Line 4   Write a four-word phrase that describes an idea or feeling about the picture.

Line 5   Write another word for the title. Use a thesaurus to help.

Da Vinci files

- Write a cinquain about a contrasting place, such as a busy street, an overcrowded beach, or a stormy sea. Choose a place you know well or find another painting to describe.

MISSION FILE 2:5

Action, space stations!

Time: To quickly escape
Place: That's up to you!

"Quick, man ze lifeboats. Ze aliens have invaded ze planet. Beam me up!"

"Calm down, Victor! The DVD you're watching isn't real, you know."

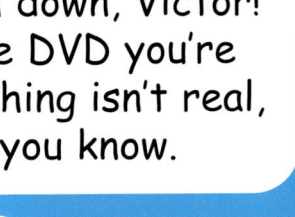

What clues can you find in this extract to show that it's the start of an action science-fiction story?

BEN RAN. An army of enemy forces swarmed towards him, attacking, charging, grabbing. A Zygun blast echoed around the metallic capsule. He spun, gripping hot steel. Another blast pounded the capsule wall. A siren screeched. He felt panic. His heart pounded. They were closing in. He darted, swerving, twisting from the grip of a Zygun guard. The door to the Cyberworld appeared before him. He knew it was his only chance ...

Work with a partner to find examples of short sentences, powerful verbs and sound effects.

What clues does the writer give to the main character's feelings?

18

Now, write the start of your own story describing someone trying to escape.

Here are some tips to get you going.

- Thought shower powerful action verbs, e.g. *spun, charged*.
- Include sound effects. Try to avoid words like bang and boom. Find synonyms (similar words) for the sounds below:

  crash   wail   cry   roar   screech   thunder

- Rather than saying the character was scared, show how they were afraid. Include phrases that describe the body reacting to fear, e.g. *his face was white, she was shaking, thoughts raced through his head.*
- Try to use short sentences.

Zat DVD was rated PG. I should have watched it vis my Muther und Farter!

Da Vinci files

- Edit your adventure to include three linked verbs that build on each other, e.g. *An army of enemy forces swarmed towards him, attacking, charging, grabbing.* This technique makes everything seem faster.
- Continue the story in the Training Mission describing Ben's escape. Include sentences with three linked verbs. Don't forget to use commas to separate the verbs.

MISSION FILE 2:6

Short but sweet

Time: Storytime
Place: Barrington Hall

"Hey Bazza, would you like to know how to keep an idiot in suspense?"

"Well of course dear boy, it would help with my creative writing."

"Okay, I'll tell you tomorrow. Heh! Heh!"

 Your mission is to write an exciting short story. Let's start by looking at how writers create suspense.

 **You can create suspense by making a character seem vulnerable. Find the meanings of the words 'suspense' and 'vulnerable'.**

Now, find synonyms (similar words) in a thesaurus.

In a short story, you should throw your reader into the action quickly.

Stick to one or two characters and a single emotion, like fear.

Short stories usually have a problem to solve.

20

"Set your story in a dark wood and include a lost character."

Lull the reader into a sense of safety. Your main character could set off with friends in daylight.

Quickly introduce the idea of being lost. Describe the weather and hint at danger, making it worse as the story goes on. Darkness could set in.

You could use rhetorical questions, e.g. *What was that moving in the shadows?*

Show the character's feelings, e.g. *His heart pounded against his chest.*

Describe what they can see and hear. Include sound effects, e.g. *an owl's screech in the dark.*

Resolve your story. The main character's friends could come to the rescue.

"Humph! Huxley's a cheeky monkey. And me, first in line to the throne!"

Da Vinci files

- Make a poster showing ways to create suspense. Start with sentences that describe the weather and season, e.g. *His breath mushroomed in front of him in the cold air.*
- Include sentences to show the character's fear and vulnerability, e.g. *Her heart pounded against her ribs. She was sweating and shaking.*
- Describe sound effects that would make the character even more afraid.
- Write lines to describe the failing light, e.g. *The darkness closed in around him.*

MISSION FILE 2:7

Buster's a bookcase ace

Time: The BA book club meeting
Place: The police station

> Man, that crime novel I've just finished sure was exciting. It was about a cereal killer on the run.

> What happened?

> He was caught after a chase with some cornflakes and a weetabix!

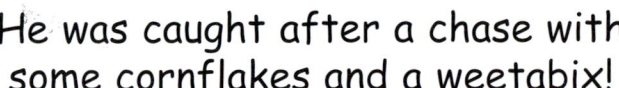 Choose a book you've read recently and make a mind map.

Start with the five Ws (who, what, why, where and when). Add other details such as characters and settings. Include a story map of the main events.

With a partner, answer these questions.

- Why would you recommend this book to a friend?
- Where does the story take place and when?
- Who is telling the story?
- What is the setting?
- What is the problem faced by the main character?
- Would you like the main character for a friend? Give your reasons.

In this mission, make sure your writing tone is appropriate for each task.

PART ONE

Your challenge is to write a review of the book you chose in the Training Mission. Include the answers to the questions you discussed.

Think about layout and format. A review of the *The Lion, the Witch and the Wardrobe* could be written inside a paper wardrobe with door flaps.

Consider style. A response to a sports book could be written as a sports commentary.

PART TWO

Now write the back cover copy to get the reader interested. Read the covers of storybooks and include the typical features below.

- A short description of the story.
- Persuasive techniques such as appealing adjectives.
- A short extract from inside. Include three full stops (an ellipsis) at the end to show there is more to follow ...
- Positive reviews, e.g. *"A thrilling read!"*
- Any awards the book has won.
- An ISBN number and the price.
- Sometimes, the back cover will tell you who drew the cover illustration.

You can see an example of a back cover on the next page.

Buster Crimes is back with a break-in to solve! He's hot on the trail of the D.A.F.T. agents ...

"A gripping read!"
The Book Review

"One of the best books of the year!"
The Storyteller

Winner of the Silver Dagger Award, 2008

Illustrations by Sandy Buckett

ISBN: 978-1-84680-363-5

£4.99

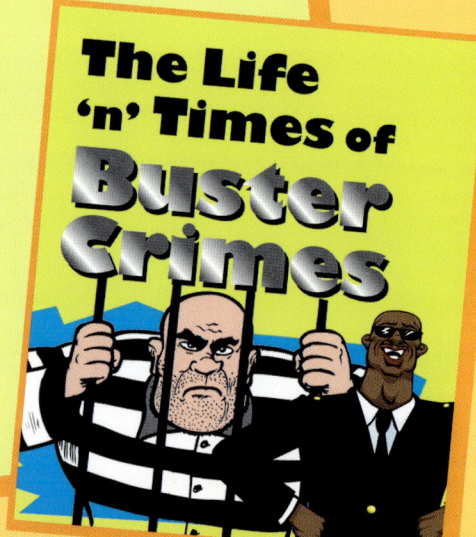

Your final task is to design the whole cover.

Fold a piece of A4 paper in half. On the front, include the title, the author's name and an illustration.

On the back, include your written copy. You could challenge yourself to completing it in no more than 50 words.

I'd like to publish a book of my police career. I'd call it *The Life 'n' Times of Buster Crimes.*

Da Vinci files

Try out some of the activities below and include them in a reading journal.

- Write a different ending for a book you've read.
- Write a short story based on characters from this book.
- Draw a map of where the story takes place and label any important places.
- Write a scene that didn't happen.
- Make a timeline of events.
- Create a diary for one of the characters.
- Write the script for a TV interview with the main character.
- Write a poem based on the book.
- Make a quiz based on a book.
- Write a letter to the main character.
- Rewrite a part of the book and include yourself as a character.
- Rewrite the story, setting it in a different time or place.
- Write a sequel (what happened after the story ended).
- Add something new to the story. You could invent something to help a character with a problem or you could change one of the events in the story.

THINK TANK 2

what makes you scared?

Are you ready for another trip into the Think Tank? Da Vinci has a new problem for you. He wants you to think about your imagination, so put on your virtual reality helmet and follow the scene carefully ...

The Scary Film

Emily pulled the cover over her head and squeezed her eyes tightly shut. It didn't work. It didn't matter what she did, the strange images came into her head and she was scared.

Emily had watched the film from behind the door, peering through a crack, unnoticed by her brother, Ryan. He was supposed to be babysitting but had got his friends to come over and watch a film. He had told Emily to go to bed and that she wasn't allowed to watch the film. It would be too scary for her and she was far too young.

Emily had wanted to prove him wrong. She had watched almost the whole film from behind the door. Now she wished she had listened to Ryan and stayed upstairs in her room.

Suddenly, Emily heard a noise. She started to cry. She knew that the monsters were just in her imagination but that the film had made them all look so real. What if just this once those monsters were real, and worse still, what if they were in her room right now!

Our imagination helps us to conjure up images in our mind. Sometimes it helps us to think of lovely faraway lands and the experience is quite nice.

At other times, our imagination plays tricks on us. Even though we know things like monsters don't exist, the images in our mind can still seem very real!

Talk about it

- What was Emily afraid of?
- Why didn't Ryan want Emily to watch the film?
- Why does Ryan think Emily is too young to watch the film?
- What could Emily do to help herself feel better?
- What is imagination? Does it create words, pictures, sounds?
- How does our imagination work?
- In what ways can our imagination be helpful?
- Can you think of how our imagination might stop us from doing something?

Write about it

- Use your imagination to describe one of the monsters Emily might have seen. Draw a picture of the monster.
- Write a story about the imaginary monsters.

Act it

- Role-play being in different places.
- Play 'Freeze frame'. Imagine you're in a jungle. When a person shouts freeze, hold position. Then imagine you are in a different setting.

MISSION FILE 2:8

Prefix mix-up ...

Time: Pre-supper
Place: The tele-vision room

"That cad Hood has mixed up all the prefixes on our computers and added them to the end of words instead of the beginning."

"How very helpful-un of him."

"Oh Huxley, he's got to you, too! Don't speak so correctly-in!"

TM

A prefix is a group of letters placed at the start of a root word to change its meaning.

Take a look at this example.

The prefix **sub-** means 'under', so a submarine goes under the sea.

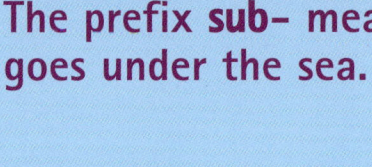

Some complicated words are easier to spell or to understand if you are familiar with prefixes.

Time yourself – you have five minutes.
How many different prefixes can you write down?

MM: Now try to find the meaning of these prefixes.

You will need a good dictionary or you can visit **dictionary.com**

photo-	ultra-	inter-	micro-
retro-	multi-	manu-	mega-
sub-	pseudo-	mal-	hydro-

Use the meaning and the prefixes to create a matching game. Make two sets of cards. On one set, write the meanings of the words and on the other, write the prefixes.

To play, lay the cards face down on a table. Ask a partner to turn over the cards two at a time and to say whether they match.

I need to stop our computers from functioning-mal. Argh! This is completely sane-in!

Da Vinci files

- Use a dictionary to work out the opposite of these words by adding a negative prefix or a prefix that means 'opposite'.

  1 necessary
  2 sane
  3 infect
  4 logical
  5 correct
  6 relevant
  7 appear
  8 septic
  9 regular
  10 legal
  11 sense
  12 mature
  13 probable
  14 spell
  15 understand
  16 similar
  17 normal
  18 symmetry

- This one is really tricky! Find the antonym (opposite) of the word 'noble', using a negative prefix.

MISSION FILE 2:9

Cat-napped?

Time: To look for poor pussykins
Place: Who knows?

"It's a CATastrophe! James is lost! I think those D.A.F.T. agents have whiskered him off somewhere. (Sniff.)"

"Don't worry, Mrs T. Huxley has some good news for you …"

"I found him in the airing cupboard having a nap. I used my word association skills – cats, nap, sleep, cosy, warm, airing cupboard!"

TM

"Now, it's your turn to use some word associations."

Play this game. Think of a word, then your partner thinks of a word with a linked meaning. Use the first word that comes to mind.

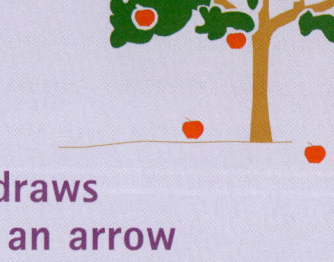

Keep going until someone pauses or repeats a word to find the winner, e.g. *green … apple … tree … plant …*

Try the same game with pictures. One person draws an object and labels it. The next person draws an arrow from the object to their associated drawing.

Some things, such as colours, have lots of associations. For example, for Hindus the colour red is associated with marriage.

Make a display of word associations. Write the word 'red', then draw pictures and write words linked in meaning around it, e.g. *danger*, *fire*, *rose*, *devils*, *Little Red Riding Hood*.

Create a shape poem. Making word associations is important for a poet to create a vivid picture. Choose a title for your poem from one of the words below:

| cello | snake | spaghetti | minibeasts | cloud |
| sunflower | swan | smash | crossroads | bridge |

Thought shower all the words linked in meaning to your title, then write a series of one-word lines in the shape of the object your poem is about.

Da Vinci files

- Write a poem entitled 'What is red?' using the word association display you made in the Main Mission.

31

MISSION FILE 2:10

Robo-hop!

Time: 'Bun' o'clock
Place: Victor's lab

"Aha! My new robo-rabbit is nearly ready for testing."

"But what does it do?"

"Ja, it acts like a normal rabbit, only you don't have to clean out ze dirty hutch!"

TM Can you help Victor design some more robo-pets?

First, put on De Bono's green hat for creative ideas and exploring alternatives. Sketch your ideas. Give your designs exciting names.

Next, wear De Bono's red hat for hunches and feelings. How do you feel about the ideas? Which one do you like the best? You don't have to give any reasons.

Ask your teacher for a handout on the **thinking skills** you need to complete this mission.

> For the main mission, write a text explaining how your robo-pet works.

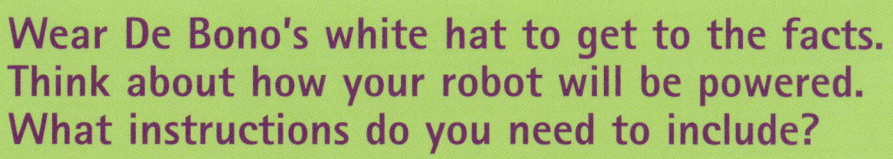

Wear De Bono's white hat to get to the facts. Think about how your robot will be powered. What instructions do you need to include?

De Bono's blue hat is for organising information. It will help you to structure your text.

- Start with a title, e.g. *How to operate the ...*
- Draw a diagram and label the technical terms.
- Write a precise description and sound informative, e.g. *The device is activated by ...*
- Use cause and effect connectives and phrases, e.g. *as a result, this causes, so, this triggers, consequently.*

Try to use subheadings for each paragraph, e.g. *What it does. What it looks like. How it works.* Include safety advice in your conclusion.

Your teacher can give you a paragraph planner to help you.

> Zis robo-rabbit is not so clean, after all. Zere is oil all over ze floor and it's eaten my 18-carot gold votch!

Da Vinci files

- Wearing De Bono's green, red, white and blue hats, create a board game aimed at 7–11 year olds. Write an explanation of how you play the game.

MISSION FILE 2:11

A cooked-up story?

Time: To get baking
Place: The Brain Academy kitchens

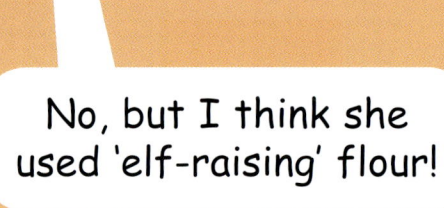

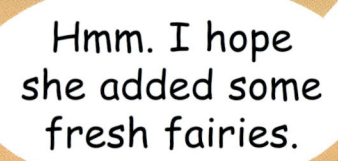

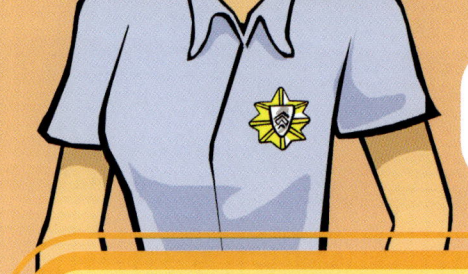

"Mrs Tiggles has made some fairy cakes for tea."

"Hmm. I hope she added some fresh fairies."

"No, but I think she used 'elf-raising' flour!"

TM: Your mission is to write a recipe for a fairy story.

Let's start by looking at these typical features of a fairy story:

- events such as weddings
- recurring phrases, e.g. *once upon a time, they lived happily ever after*
- themes, including good versus evil, magic, things in groups of three or seven
- faraway lands and timeless settings
- stereotypical characters that provide a quick identity but ignore the uniqueness of individuals

34

> A recipe is an instructional text. So, let's think how to write good instructions.

Your instructions should include:

- a title and list of ingredients
- a method in chronological (time) order using imperatives (order verbs), e.g. *mix*, *blend*
- a clear layout with a heading for each section and bulleted or numbered points
- precise instructions using adverbs, e.g. *carefully*, *slowly*, and short clear sentences

Now, write your recipe for a fairy story following the plan below.

1. Thought shower imperative verbs, adverbs and containers, e.g. *jar*, *box*, *tube*.
2. Include a heading, e.g. *Recipe for a Fairy Story*.
3. Bullet point your ingredients and use precise adjectives, e.g. *three spoonfuls of fairy magic*.
4. Number each step in your method and start with an imperative. Here is an example.
   1. *Take a princess and dress her in rags.*
   2. *Stir in an evil stepmother to break up a romance.*

> Ah, dear James has licked the bowl clean. No need to wash up now!

Da Vinci files

- Choose a traditional fairy story such as *Cinderella* and rewrite the ending. As an alternative, mix together the characters from more than one fairy story to make a new tale.

MISSION FILE 2:12

Liquid all-sports

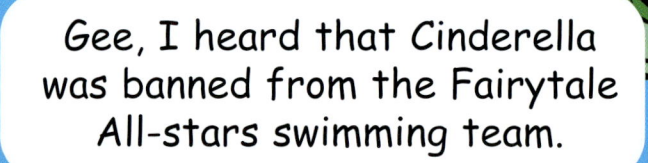

Time: A summer afternoon
Place: The Brain Academy swimming gala

"Gee, I heard that Cinderella was banned from the Fairytale All-stars swimming team."

"Really Tex, why's that?"

"She was wearing glass flippers!"

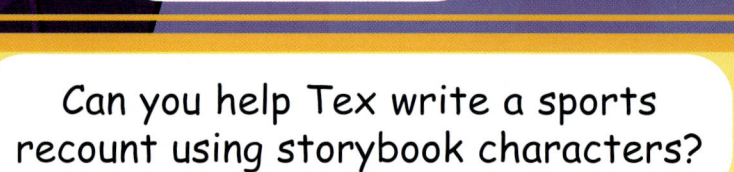

TM

"Can you help Tex write a sports recount using storybook characters?"

Sports recounts are similar to other newspaper reports. First decide on a sport. It could be football, netball or even an egg and spoon race.

Next, think of storybook characters that could appear such as Harry Potter or Winnie the Pooh.

Make up a short headline to hook your reader, e.g. *Winnie wins gold*.

Here are some more tips to help you.

In your opening paragraph, explain:
- who is involved
- where
- what happened
- when

E.g. *Winnie the Pooh beat Tigger to win the Eastern Region honey hunt in Cambridge, yesterday.*

Sports recounts often include time adverbials. Thought shower time adverbials to start each paragraph, e.g. *in the opening lap, in the second half, in the final minutes.*

Next, choose events to include. You could describe goals, cheating and accidents. Decide what happens first, next and at the end.

Write a quotation for your final paragraph to give the story a personal angle. Here is an example:

"*It was a great challenge but the prize was worth it,*" *smiled Winnie the Pooh.*

Da Vinci files

- Newspaper reports often use parenthetic commas. These are commas around an added piece of information.

  Try writing sentences about book characters using parenthetic commas, e.g. *Tigger, the bouncy tiger, tripped on the final hurdle.*

MISSION FILE 2:13

Book a table fast!

Time: Supper time
Place: Barrington Hall

"I'm opening a restaurant. All the proceeds will go to my new charity P.A.U.N.C.H. (**P**arents **a**gainst **u**nhealthy **c**hildren's **h**urried meals.)"

"Posh nosh – leg of salmon and lobster, soup in a basket. Haw! Haw!"

"That's great, your highness. What's on the menu?"

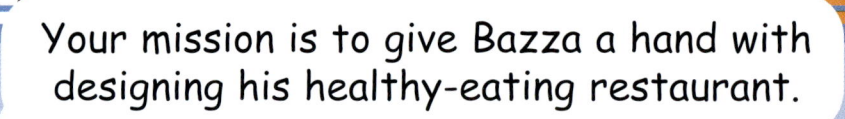

TM

"Your mission is to give Bazza a hand with designing his healthy-eating restaurant.

What would you like in your ideal healthy restaurant?

Decide how to make it different, such as waiters in top hats, fruit baskets on display.

Sketch your options. Be as creative as you can.

Use De Bono's technique PO. This means saying something to see what it sets off in your mind. Consider these words to stimulate new ideas:

| choice | comfort | movement | entertainment |
| light | serving | safety | technology |

Ask your teacher for a handout on the **thinking skills** you need to complete this mission.

Now, write a menu for the restaurant.

Give the place a catchy title. Try to use alliteration. That's where several words start with the same letter, e.g. *Bazza's Beanburger Bar*.

Make a list of exciting meals and drinks to put on the menu.

Thought shower appealing adjectives, e.g. *scrumptious*, *lip-smacking*. Use a thesaurus or visit thesaurus.com to help you.

You could even create your menu around a theme such as magic and offer Ghost burgers!

Design the menu attractively on paper or a computer. Include your theme in the design.

Describe a special offer.

A customer complained the coffee tasted like dirt. I explained I had only 'ground' it this morning!

Da Vinci files

- Write an advert for the opening of the restaurant. Consider why its design is suited to healthy eating. What makes it exciting and different? How is it themed?
- Try to include persuasive techniques such as imperatives (order verbs), e.g. *relax*, *enjoy*. Use appealing adjectives to describe the foods and special offers.

MISSION FILE 2:14

Here be dragons!

Time: Drags-on sometimes
Place: The Dragon's den

"I wanted a pet dragon once. Cute as a pup but they grow up to be very grumpy and have smelly breath."

"You are joking aren't you, Echo?"

"Well sort of, although there are REAL dragons living on the island of Komodo! Take a look on the Internet."

"Your mission is to invent a dragon for Echo and write a report about it."

Structure your report using the table below.

Appearance	Describe its size, features and lifespan. Is it developed from or similar to any other species?
Diet	Are there any special foods it eats?
Enemies	Does it have any? Who are they? Is it the prey of another creature?
Habitat	What environment does it live in?
Character	Use similes to describe its character, e.g. it is as large as, it is as fearsome as …

Now, sketch your dragon and label any special features with a ruler and a pencil.

long snout to heat up fire breath

wings for flying over mountains

claws for digging up food

Let's imagine your dragon is endangered. It is kept in a special conservation area to encourage breeding.

Your task is to write a Dragon Handbook. It should be an explanatory guide on how to look after the creature and how to keep the species alive.

Below are some of the questions you should answer in the book.

- What do you need to look after the dragon?
- What is the best diet for the dragon?
- What should you provide to stop it from getting bored?

Dragon

MM Use headings to split up different sections of information, e.g. *Safety with Dragons*, *Dragon Diet*.

Try to use causal connectives, e.g. *consequently*, *in order to*, *as a result*. These show how one action leads to another and what may happen. Here is an example.

Make sure the dragon has plenty of coal to chew; consequently, it will be able to breathe fire. Provide it with a special area for firebreathing in order to avoid accidents.

If I had a pet dragon, I'd be able to use my hosepipes to put out any accidental fires!

Da Vinci files

Choose activities from this list as part of a project on dragons.

- Write instructions on how to catch a dragon.
- Write an acrostic poem about a dragon. That's a poem where each line begins with a letter from the word 'dragon'.
- Write a story that starts like this: When everything was young, the dragons were the guardians of the Earth.
- Write a newspaper article with the headline 'The Dragons are back'.
- Research and write about Chinese dragons.
- Write a legend entitled 'How the dragon got its wings'.
- Write a cookery book for a dragon.
- Create a wanted poster for a dragon.

MISSION FILE 2:15

The Scottish Play

Time: Opening night
Place: The Brain Academy theatre

"Remember, it's bad luck in the theatre to say the name of this play by Shakespeare."

"Golly-gee DV, I thought Macbeth was the name of another hamburger joint."

"Arghh! He's said the name Macbeth! Arghh, so have I!!"

TM

Let's take a closer look at the imagery in the play.

Similes and metaphors are word pictures. They help to create images in your mind.

A simile is a comparison. It puts together two things that have a likeness. It explains that one thing is **like** another thing.

A metaphor demands we use our imagination. It says that something **is** another thing.

44

Now, it's your turn to draw some word pictures and answer a few questions.

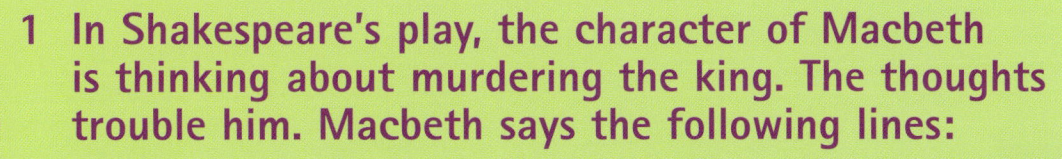

1. In Shakespeare's play, the character of Macbeth is thinking about murdering the king. The thoughts trouble him. Macbeth says the following lines:

   O full of scorpions is my mind, dear wife.

   Draw this image (word picture). What do you think he means?

2. Later, when Macbeth decides to carry out the murder, he says:

   *... look like the innocent flower,
   But be the serpent under't.*

   Draw this image. What do you think he means when he says this line?

Da Vinci files

- In his play *As You Like It*, Shakespeare uses another metaphor:

  *All the World's a stage,
  And all the men and women merely players:
  They have their exits and their entrances;
  And one man in his time plays many parts,
  His acts being seven ages.*

- What is the more common name for the job that 'players' do today?

- What do you think the fourth line of the metaphor means?

- Rewrite this passage using a different metaphor, e.g. All the world's a book ... or a zoo, a supermarket, a museum, a game ...

THINK TANK 3

What is happiness?

This is your final trip into the Think Tank. The problem Da Vinci has set will make you think about the nature of happiness. Put on your virtual reality helmet and follow the scene carefully …

The Poetry Lesson

TJ listened carefully to what he had to do. This week, they had been looking at different types of poetry and TJ had loved it! They had looked at what the words meant, broken down the rhyming patterns and talked about their favourite poems. Usually, TJ hated anything to do with reading and writing but, somehow, looking at the poems had seemed so much easier.

The teacher turned the page of the book to reveal what they would be doing today. It was a poem called 'Happiness'. He sat back and listened carefully as his teacher brought the words on the page to life.

"Now, think about what makes you happy," instructed his teacher, "and use this poem to help you to write your own."

TJ sat in his place, turned to a clean page and thought carefully. He looked over to where Dana was sitting and saw some of the things on her list. She had written down eating sweets, playing the guitar and reading. That didn't help – he didn't know how anyone could enjoy doing those things!

TJ knew what he liked to do – playing on the computer, drawing, dancing but did these things really make him happy or did he just like doing them? And what did being happy feel like anyway?

Happiness means different things to different people. Some people feel happy when the sun shines or when they are with people they love. Other people are happy on holiday or eating their favourite foods.

There is no one particular thing that makes everyone happy. Everyone is unique, so different things make different people happy.

Talk about it

- How do different things make different people happy?
- Why did Dana and TJ have different things on their lists?
- What does it feel like to be happy?
- What makes you happy?
- What did TJ find difficult about writing the poem?
- What is happiness?

Write about it

- Thought shower things that make you feel happy.
- Compare your thought shower with a partner's work. Do the same things or different things make you feel happy?
- Write a list poem about things that make you feel happy.

Act it

- A world where everyone is happy all the time.
- A world where nothing makes anyone happy.
- Talking to TJ to help him find out what makes him feel happy.

The TASC Problem Solving Wheel

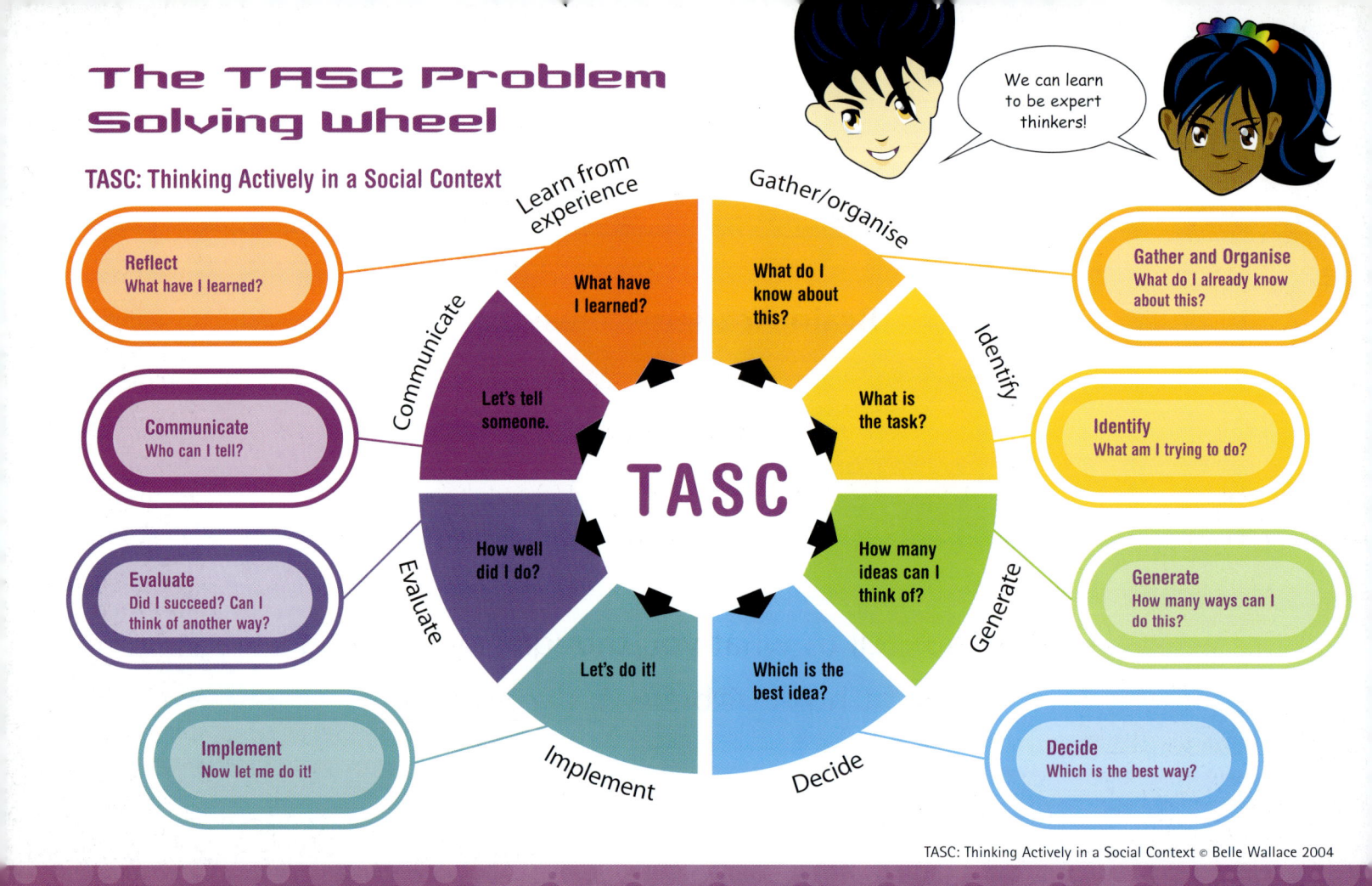

TASC: Thinking Actively in a Social Context

We can learn to be expert thinkers!

Wheel segments (clockwise from top):
- Learn from experience — What have I learned?
- Gather/organise — What do I know about this?
- Identify — What is the task?
- Generate — How many ideas can I think of?
- Decide — Which is the best idea?
- Implement — Let's do it!
- Evaluate — How well did I do?
- Communicate — Let's tell someone.

Reflect — What have I learned?
Gather and Organise — What do I already know about this?
Identify — What am I trying to do?
Generate — How many ways can I do this?
Decide — Which is the best way?
Implement — Now let me do it!
Evaluate — Did I succeed? Can I think of another way?
Communicate — Who can I tell?

TASC: Thinking Actively in a Social Context © Belle Wallace 2004

nace

What is NACE?

NACE is a charity which was set up in 1984. It is an organisation that supports the teaching of 'more able' pupils and helps all children find out what they are good at and to do their best.

What does NACE do?

NACE helps teachers by giving them advice, books, materials and training.
Many teachers, headteachers, parents and governors join NACE. Members of NACE can use a special website which gives them useful advice, ideas and materials to help children to learn.

NACE helps thousands of schools and teachers every year. It also helps teachers and children in other countries, such as America and China.

How will this book help me?

Brain Academy English books challenge and help you to become better at learning by:
- Making you think critically about information
- Encouraging you to solve problems creatively
- Helping you to generate new ideas and make decisions
- Encouraging you to make connections to what you already know
- Letting you make mistakes and learn from them
- Asking you to work with your teacher, by yourself and with others
- Expecting you to get better and to go on to the next book
- Developing skills you can use in other subjects and out of school

We hope that you enjoy the books!

Write to **RISING STARS** and let us know how the books helped you to learn and what you would like to see in the next books.

Rising Stars UK Ltd, 22 Grafton Street, London W1S 4EX